Table of Contents

MW00907642

Ode to Joy

Ode to Joy

German Dance

Melody

German Dance

Harmony

Gypsy Love Song

Melody

Gypsy Love Song

Harmony

mp

mf

mp

8

America, the Beautiful

Melody

America, the Beautiful

Harmony

Italian Song

Melody

mf

Italian song

Patriotic March

12

Melody

Patriotic March

Long, Long Ago

Long, Long Ago

Skater's Waltz

Melody

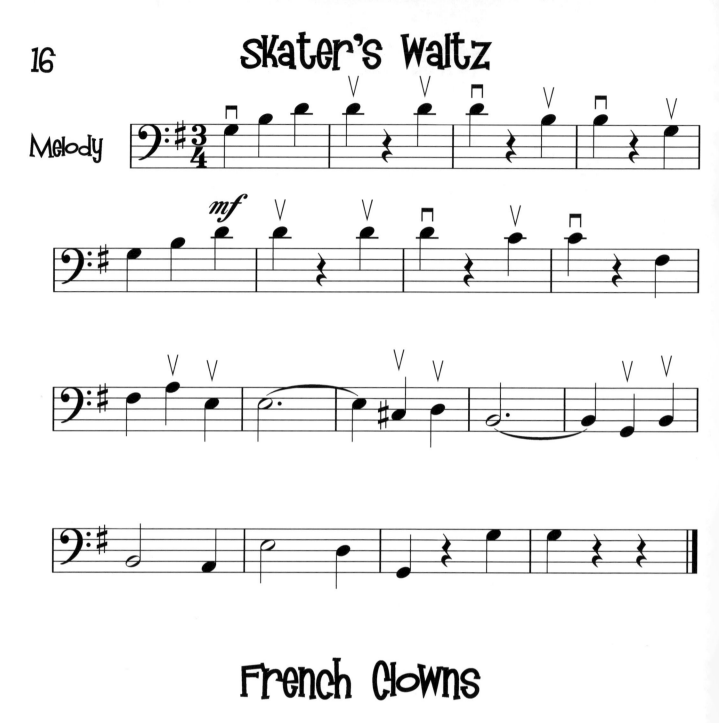

French Clowns

Melody

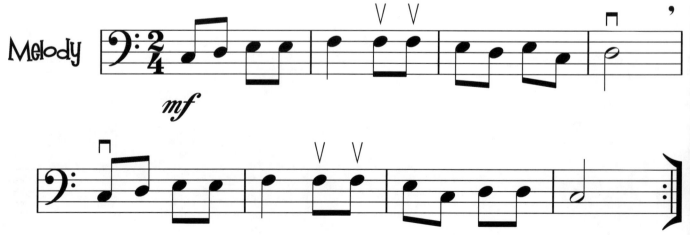

Skater's Waltz

Harmony

French Clowns

Harmony

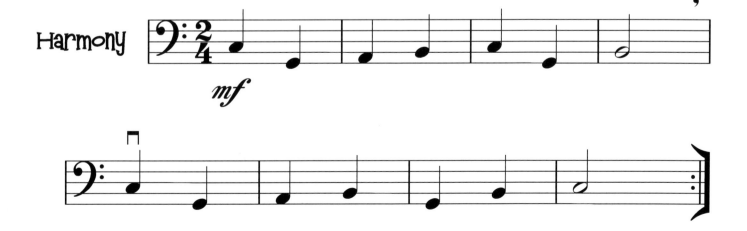

18 Latin Dancers

see, the Conquering Hero Comes

Latin Dancers

see, the Conquering Hero Comes

20

Fight song

Melody

Fight song

Harmony

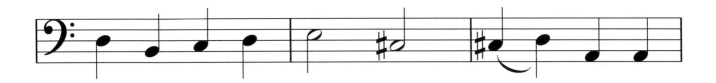

surprise symphony

22

Melody

surprise symphony

Mozart's Theme in C

Mozart's Theme in C

Harmony

March

Fine

Melody

D.C. al Fine

March

Haydn's Waltz

Haydn's Waltz

To a Wild Rose

To a Wild Rose

Harmony

Haydn's Anthem

Melody

Haydn's Anthem

Mozart's Theme in D

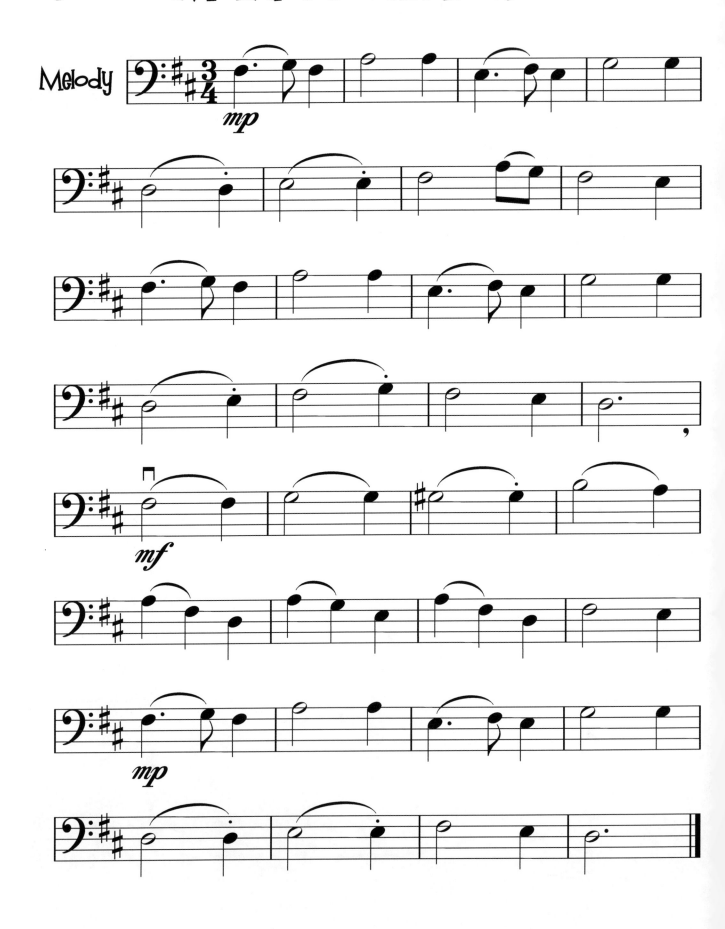

Mozart's Theme in D

Harmony

Aura Lee

Aura Lee

Kum Bah Yah

Melody

Kum Bah Yah

Harmony

Trumpet Voluntary

Chorale

Trumpet Voluntary

Harmony

Chorale

Harmony

Rigadoon

Rigadoon

Camptown Races

Melody

Camptown Races

Mozart Processional

Mozart Processional

Harmony

Amazing Grace

Amazing Grace

Skip to My Lou

50

Skip to My Lou

Home on the Range

Melody

Home on the Range

Harmony

Brahm's Lullaby

Melody

Brahm's Lullaby

Harmony

Chester

Melody

Chester

The King's March

The King's March

60 Go, Fight, Win!

Melody

Go, Fight, Win!

Harmony

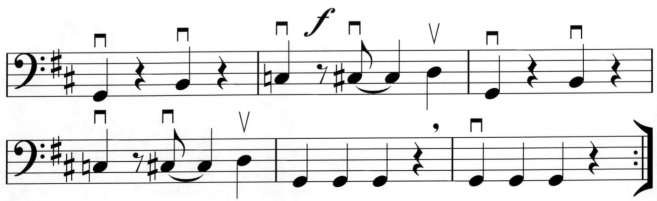

Made in United States
Orlando, FL
15 December 2023

41072419R00035